Orca Pup's Escape

SEA ANIMALS MINI BOOK

For Tara, who reminded me how difficult it is to allow what is natural and shy
of civilization to remain so. — M.A.

To Morgan. — K.L.

©2002 Studio Mouse, and the Smithsonian Institution, Washington, D.C. 20560 U

Published by McGraw-Hill Children's Publishing, a Division of The McGraw-Hill
Companies.

Send all inquiries to:
McGraw-Hill Children's Publishing • 8787 Orion Place • Columbus, Ohio 43240

ISBN 1-58845-416-9

1 2 3 4 5 6 7 8 9 10 CHRT 08 07 06 05 04 03 02 01

Printed in China.

Acknowledgments:
Our very special thanks to Dr. Charles Handley of the Department of Vertebrate Zoology at the Smithsonian's
National Museum of Natural History for his curatorial review.

Orca Pup's Escape

by Michael C. Armour   Illustrated by Katie Lee

McGraw-Hill
Children's Publishing

As a rosy sun settles over the sea, eight orca whales—the greatest and most powerful hunters in all the oceans of the world—leap up the coast.

5

Young Orca Pup sings and
splashes at the rear of the group, as
the ocras slip quickly into the net to
feed before the fishermen notice.

8

As Orca Pup turns away from the group to catch a juicy salmon nearby, a storm of fishing boats close in, sending the orca pod racing away to safety.

11

Orca Pup's dorsal fin is caught in an abandoned cargo net! He bucks and thrashes until he is nearly out of breath, and too tired to move or call out to his pod.

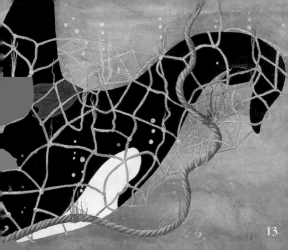

Orca Pup strains at the net with his muscles and cuts it with his teeth, trying one more time to break free. The ropes snap and Orca Pup rushes to the surface for air.

Tired after the long fight and away from his pod for the first time, Orca Pup drifts half-asleep through the lonely moonlit seas.

Dawn chases the moon out of the sky.
Shadowy hills glide by as Orca Pup drifts
closer and closer to land.

Orca Pup wakes to find himself beached on the shore, with a sandbar between him and the sea, where he belongs, and the sun's heat beating on his back.

31

About the Orca Whale

Weighing from four to ten tons, orca whales are warm-blooded, air-breathing mammals that grow up to 30 feet long and can live as long as 50 years. Orcas travel in pods and have no natural enemies, apart from humans. Orca pups have lifelong ties to their mothers, usually swimming no more than 100 yards from their sides. Orcas are well-known for their acrobatic abilities and are able to perform tricks such as spy hops, flipper slaps, belly whops, spiraling breaches, and barrel rolls.

Orca Pup hears strange sounds around him and feels a soft tickling on his back. He is being pushed back into the cool water of the sea.

Orca Pup dives down into a kelp forest and finds a school of herring to eat, but he is not yet a good hunter and frightens the fish away with his noise.

Still searching for his family, Orca Pup sees three humpback whales rising through the water, and hears their whistling songs.

Through the slow songs of the humpback, Orca Pup hears another song—an orca song—and breaks through the water's surface, searching for a sign of his pod.

Against the sun, Orca Pup sees his family rising out of the waves coming toward him. He races toward their familiar song.